Dedicated to my beloved sons, Samuel and Steven, whose endless wonder and creativity catalyzed the creation of this book. May it continue to bring joy and inspiration to you both until the day you share it with your own little ones.

Enjoy this story of love, family and cultural heritage.

Sheeba
2024

Publisher - Sheeba Varghese
Book Cover and Illustrations- Tori Tilahun
Formatted and Printed by Babooky

Title: Mommy, Am I Indian Today?
By Sheeba Varghese

ISBN: 978 1 7354342 1 6

TO GET IN TOUCH:
Email: sheebad72@gmail.com
Visit: www.sheebavarghese.com

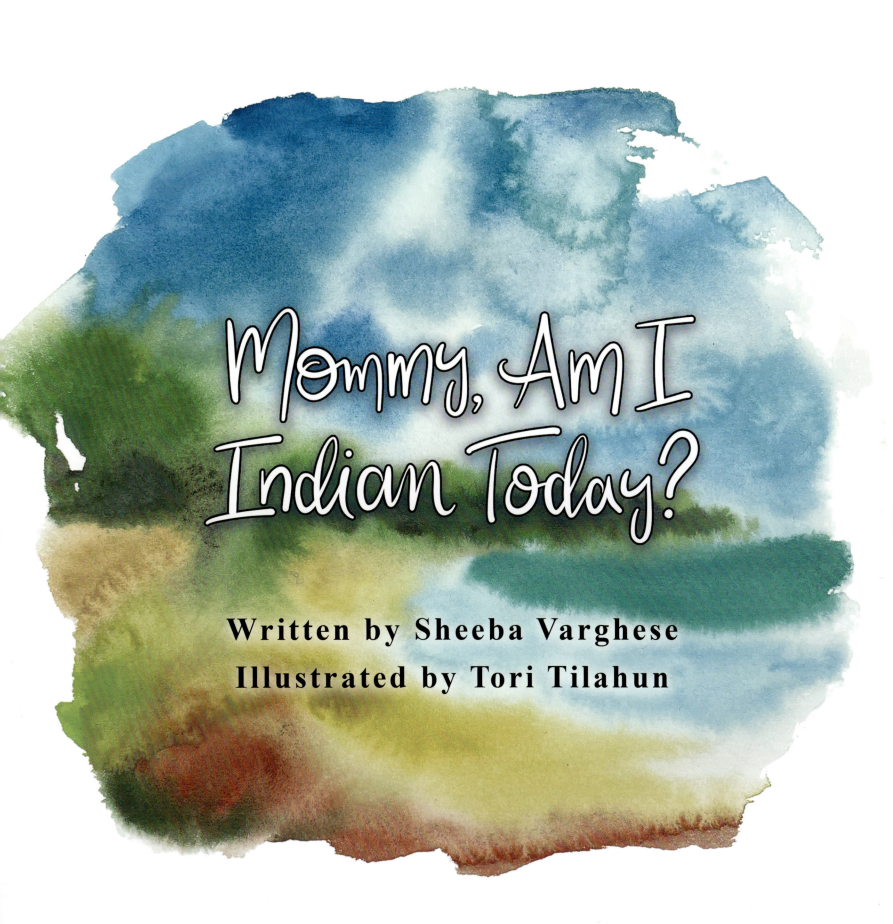

Mommy, Am I Indian Today?

Written by Sheeba Varghese

Illustrated by Tori Tilahun

"Hurry up, boys, we need to
get ready for the wedding," Mom called out.

As usual, Mom had these funny outfits that we only wore on special occasions like weddings, parties, and "big" people events.

I actually thought I looked pretty cool when I wore them. The pants were a bit harder to wear because of the strings that I had to pull, and the shirt was a bit long and could be very itchy at times.

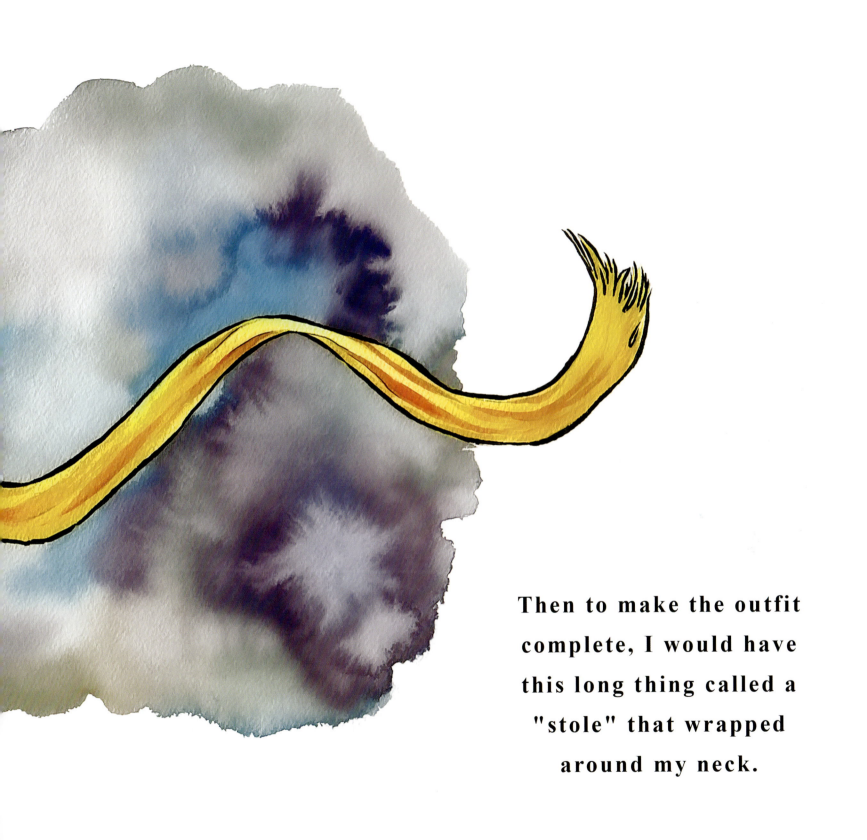

Then to make the outfit complete, I would have this long thing called a "stole" that wrapped around my neck.

My brother and I always matched whenever we wore our outfits.

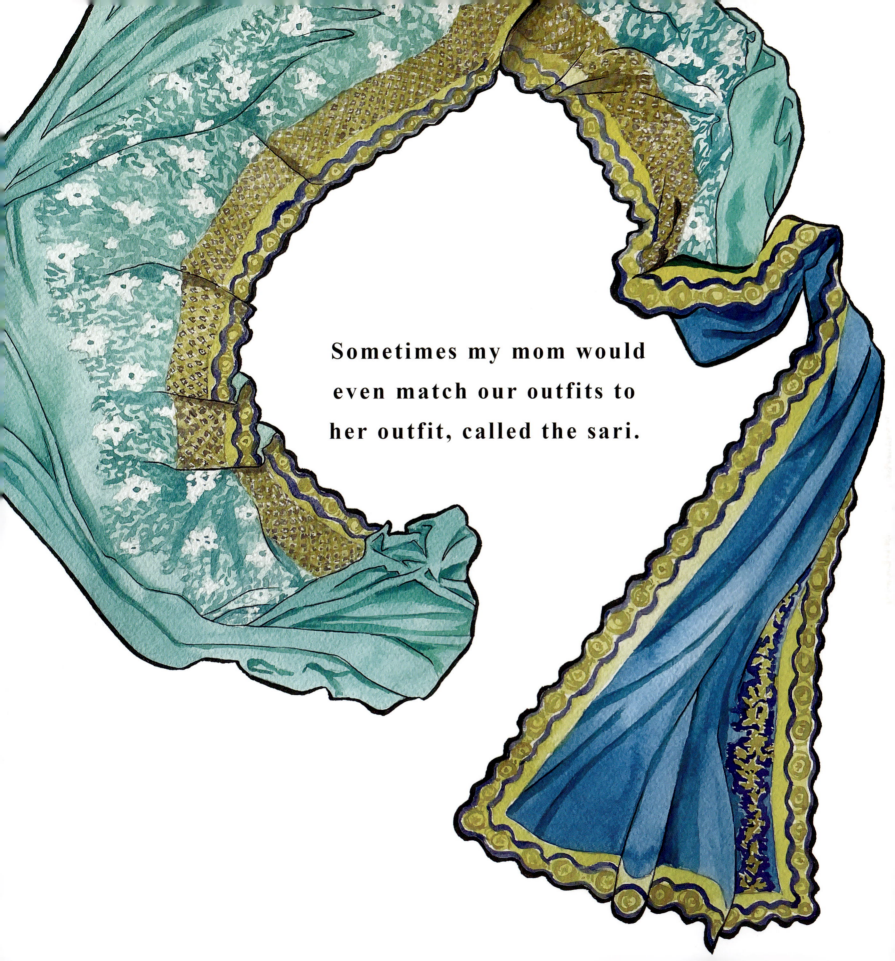

Sometimes my mom would even match our outfits to her outfit, called the sari.

As my mom was helping me get dressed, I asked her, "Mommy, am I Indian today?" For some reason, she thought it was a funny question.

She took out this huge album from the bookcase and began to explain the story of her parents coming to America . . .

. . .many, many years ago.

As she showed me all the pictures, she said, "Well, honey, you were born in the United States, but your parents and your grandparents were born in India."

"Although there are many states in India, much of your family grew up in the state of Kerala."

"It wasn't easy for them as they left the comforts of their home to come to America in search of a better life and opportunities for their children.

They endured many hard times, and we are incredibly grateful for all the sacrifices they made for each of us."

"So, no... we are not just Indians today when we wear these fancy clothes. We are Indians every day."

I smiled at her and felt even more special as I walked out the door in my traditional Indian outfit, called the kurta pyjama.

I extend my heartfelt gratitude to my husband, Santosh, whose unwavering love and support made this project a reality. Your encouragement has been a constant in my life, and I am endlessly grateful for your belief in me.

To Tori, the illustrator I've been searching for, your collaboration has brought immense joy to this journey. Your creativity and dedication have breathed life into the pages of this book.

To my family and friends, natural and spiritual, your endless encouragement have been my greatest blessings. Thank you for standing by me and inspiring me to pursue my dreams.

Lastly, I am deeply thankful to God for the gift of life and creativity. Your gentle whispers have guided me through this process, turning ordinary moments into beautiful stories. Thank you, Lord, for the inspiration and grace that flow abundantly from your hand.

In the vibrant Bay Area of San Francisco, Sheeba Varghese resides with her husband, Santosh, where they indulge in fine dining, embark on exciting adventures around the globe, and cheer passionately for their basketball team, the Warriors. As the CEO & Founder of Defining Moments 365 LLC, she leads a coaching consultancy dedicated to leadership training and coaching. A defining moment in her life sparked a profound desire to create children's books, fueled by her love for simplicity and her experiences raising her own children, now adults. Through her stories, she seeks to impart valuable lessons and spread joy to the younger generation of readers.

Tori Tilahun has been drawing and painting ever since she could hold a paintbrush. She studied to learn oil painting under Patty Hutchens then began painting in watercolor in 2014. Since then she has completely fallen in love with the media, focusing mostly on developing a unique style of combining highly detailed portraiture and loose watercolor blooms. You'll often find her lost in the details of a painting in her studio in Leesburg, Virginia, or lost hiking in the woods and trails along the Potomac River with her husband and two kids.